The Word Hunter's
Companion

ENGLISH DEPARTMENT
AYLWIN SCHOOL

The Word Hunter's Companion

A First Thesaurus

JAMES GREEN
Assisted by ARTHUR THOMAS

BASIL BLACKWELL · OXFORD

0 631 93890 7 (Paper)
0 631 17380 3 (Cased)

Reprinted March and October 1977
Reprinted 1979, 1981, 1982, 1983, 1984

Printed and bound in Great Britain at
The Camelot Press Ltd, Southampton

How to Use This Book

When you are writing it is sometimes difficult to find or to remember the word which will say exactly what you mean, and so you may use a word which is easy to remember but which is not really right.

In this book there are numbered words in **Bold type** called 'key-words'. These are probably words you use very often. Underneath each key-word is a list of words that can sometimes be used instead of the key-word. Alongside some, meanings are explained, so you should be able to choose exactly the word you need.

Words without explanation immediately below a key-word mean the same as the key-word itself.

Use the index at the end of the book to find the word you were thinking of using, then look up the number given and choose what you think is the best word for your purpose.

You will find some extra words printed in *italics*. A dictionary or special reference-book may help you with these.

Nouns

1 all

everyone   everything

everybody	All people.
the sum	All the parts added together.
the total	The full amount.
the whole	All together with nothing missing, the sum of all the parts.

2 animal

amphibian	An animal able to live on land and in water.
beast	Any four-legged animal.
bird	A feathered animal with wings.
creature	Any person or animal living or dead.
fish	An animal living in water and breathing through gills.
insect	A small six-legged creature with its body in three parts.
mammal	An animal which suckles its young.
monster	A large and unusual beast.
pet	A tame animal kept for pleasure.
reptile	A scaly, cold-blooded animal which creeps on very short legs or on its belly.
rodent	An animal with front teeth specially suited for gnawing.
vermin	(a) Animals which harm crops or prey on game.
	(b) Fleas, lice, bedbugs, etc. [Notice that 'vermin' is always plural.]

3 answer

reply   response

excuse	An explanation to avoid blame.
explanation	A statement making something clear.
retort	A reply flung back at once.
solution	An explanation of a problem.
rejoinder riposte.	

4 baby

brat	A child disliked for some reason.
cherub	A happy baby with chubby cheeks like those of an angel child.
child	A very young person.
infant	A young child.
toddler	A small child who walks with short unsteady steps.
tot	A very small child.
bairn	

5 bag

briefcase	A small stiff case mostly used for carrying papers.
case	A stiff rectangular container used for carrying belongings.
duffelbag	A bag of coarse strong cloth closed by a drawn string at the top.
handbag	A small bag carried by women.
haversack	A canvas bag with straps used for carrying food.
holdall	A zipped case of loose material with two large strap handles.
rucksack	A canvas bag carried on the back, with straps over both shoulders.
sack	An open-topped container of coarse material.
saddlebag	A bag carried across a horse or at the back of a bicycle.
satchel	A leather or plastic case used by schoolchildren.
suitcase	A large case used for carrying clothes.
portfolio	

6 ball

sphere

globe	An object appearing round from all directions.

7 boat

craft   vessel

canoe	A lightweight boat moved by paddling.
coaster	A cargo boat which travels along the coast.
dinghy	(a) an inflatable boat. (b) a small rowing boat.
ferry-boat	A boat used to carry people or goods across a stretch of water.
galleon	A large ancient sailing ship of several decks with high bow and stern.
galley	An ancient ship moved by oars and sails, often worked by slaves or convicts.
launch	A large motor-driven boat used for pleasure or patrol.
schooner	A fore-and-aft rigged vessel usually with two or three masts.
submarine	A vessel designed to travel on or below the surface of the sea.
tender	A small vessel attending a larger one.
tug	A small powerful boat used to tow larger boats.
yacht	(a) a light sailing vessel specially designed for racing. (b) a powered luxury vessel built for pleasure-cruising.

drifter   *trawler*

8 book

album	(a) A book with blank pages in which a collection of items may be formed. (b) A collection of printed music or pictures in book form.
anthology	A collection of writings by various authors.
atlas	A collection of maps.
classic	A work of literature of lasting merit.
diary	(a) A book prepared for making day to day records. (b) An account of the day to day life of the writer.
dictionary	A collection of words in alphabetical order, with their meanings.
encyclopaedia	A work, in one or more volumes, giving information about many subjects.
handbook	A convenient book of instructions.
log	A record of events especially those on a sea voyage.
manual	As for Handbook.
manuscript	(a) Typed or written work which an author sends to a publisher.

	(b) A handwritten book sometimes decorated.
novel	A book telling a story of imaginary people and events.
paperback	A book with paper covers.
publication	A printed book, magazine or paper issued in quantity.
textbook	A book of instruction dealing with a special subject for study in school or college.
thriller	An exciting book, a story of crime, detection or mystery.
tome	A very heavy book, often old or dull.
volume	(a) A book as one of a set or series.
	(b) As for Book.
thesaurus	

9 box

cabinet	A cupboard made of wood or metal, and sometimes glass, often used for display.
caddy	A metal or plastic container for storing tea.
carton	A cardboard container.
case	A frame with glass, leather or wooden sides used for protection.
casket	A small box of fine workmanship for jewellery or trinkets.
chest	A large wooden box, sometimes bound with metal straps with a hinged lid.
container	Any article in which something can be held.
crate	A large wooden container used to protect things when they travel.
locker	A box or small cupboard usually fitted with a lock and key.
safe	A metal container with strong locks for storing valuables.
strong-box	A metal box, which can be securely locked, for storing valuables.
trunk	A box of wood or leather or metal, with hinged lid and used for travelling.
locket	

10 boy

lad

adolescent	A person soon to become an adult.
child	Someone older than a baby but not yet grown up.

juvenile	A person not yet an adult in the eyes of the law.
minor	A person below the age of 18.
schoolboy	A boy who attends school.
stripling	A thin young man.
teenager	A person aged over 12 but not yet 20.
urchin	A poor boy of ragged appearance.
youngster	A lively young person.
youth	A young man.

11 bus

coach	A single-deck passenger vehicle.
double-decker	A bus with upper and lower deck.
minicoach	A vehicle for a small group of people usually not more than twelve.
tram	A public vehicle driven by electricity or steam or drawn by horses along rails in a road.
trolley-bus	A bus powered by electricity from overhead cables.

12 car

automobile

convertible	A car with a roof which can be put up and taken down.
coupé	A closed two-seater car.
hearse	A large funeral vehicle used for carrying the coffin.
jalopy	An old car in poor condition.
jeep	A strong open vehicle developed by the U.S. armed forces for rough ground.
limousine	A large luxury motor car.
racing-car	A very powerful car designed especially for racing.
saloon	A car with fixed roof and sides for more than two people.
sports car	A fast powerful car designed for road use.
taxi	A car with driver and available for hire in the street.

13 chair

armchair	A chair with supports for the arms.
bench	A long seat without arms or back usually of wood.

couch	A long low padded seat on which to sit or lie.
deckchair	A collapsible canvas chair with a wooden or metal frame.
pew	A long wooden seat for members of a church or chapel congregation.
rocking-chair	A chair designed to rock backwards and forwards.
seat	Anything to sit on.
settee	An upholstered seat for two or more persons.
settle	A long high-backed wooden seat.
sofa	A large padded couch with a raised back.
stool	A backless seat for one person.
throne	The ceremonial chair for a king, a bishop or other person of high rank.

14 city

borough	A town with its own council.
burgh	A Scottish Borough.
metropolis	The chief town in a country or region.
port	A town with a harbour.
suburb	An outlying part of a town or city.
town	A place with more people than a village but not created a city.

15 coat

anorak	A hooded waterproof jacket.
cloak	A long loose outer garment draped from the shoulders.
duffelcoat	A hooded coat of heavy duffel cloth.
greatcoat	A heavy overcoat.
jerkin	A short close-fitting sleeveless jacket of leather or strong material.
mac	A lightweight waterproof overcoat.
macintosh	As for Mac.
overcoat	A long coat worn out of doors over indoor clothing.
parka	A hooded windproof outer jacket.
plastic mac	A rainproof coat of plastic, easily folded away.

16 crowd

bunch	A closely-packed company of people.
crush	A tightly-packed mass of people.
group	A number of people sharing views, social customs, beliefs, etc.
horde	A large disorderly, threatening crowd.
host	A very large crowd or army.
huddle	A confused bunch of people.
mob	A lawless and excited crowd.
multitude	A very great number of people.
rabble	A noisy uncontrolled crowd.
throng	A large closely-packed crowd of people.

audience   congregation   galaxy

17 drink

mouthful	Enough to fill the mouth.
nightcap	A drink taken before going to bed at night.
nip	A small drink.
pint	A drink from a tankard or glass holding a pint.
sip	A small quantity taken by the lips.
swig	A large amount taken in a long drawn-out drink.
taste	A very small quantity.
toast	A drink in honour of someone or something.
tot	As for Nip.

draught   tipple

18 farm

croft	A small Scottish farm in the Highlands or Isles.
market-garden	A place especially set out for growing fruit and vegetables to be sold.
ranch	A very large farm mainly for grazing cattle.
smallholding	A very small farm.

19 fight

affray	A scrambling, untidy outbreak of fighting.
battle	A large-scale fight between military forces.
combat	A struggle between two people or two forces.
conflict	A violent disagreement between sides.
dogfight	A fight between enemy war planes chasing and dodging each other.
feud	A persistent quarrel leading to outbreaks of fighting often between clans or families.
melée	As for Affray.
scrap	A small, unexpected fight.
scuffle	A small, untidy, confused struggle.
skirmish	A hasty fight between small groups from two rival forces.
war	A major struggle between nations or groups of nations.

blitz   campaign   duel   scrimmage   shindy   tussle

20 fire

beacon	A signal-fire on high ground.
blaze	A fire burning furiously.
bonfire	(a) a garden fire for burning rubbish.
	(b) an outdoor fire built for a celebration.
conflagration	A large destructive fire.

21 friend

chum

acquaintance	A person whom one knows slightly.
ally	Someone who co-operates, supporting in a plan of action.
companion	Someone who spends much time in the company of another.
comrade	A close companion and supporter.
crony	An old close friend.
mate	A fellow-worker.

associate   colleague   fan   neighbour   partner   patron

22 game

competition	A test of skill between contestants.
contest	As for Competition.
event	One of the parts of a competition.
match	A competition between two equal sides.
rally	A large meeting.
sports	A collection of competitive events.
tournament	(a) A series of contests often taking several days.
	(b) A medieval contest.

23 garden

allotment	One of several plots of ground rented for gardening.
flower-garden	A garden for growing flowers.
kitchen-garden	A garden for growing vegetables for a household.
market-garden	A garden in which vegetables and fruit are grown for sale.
orchard	A collection of fruit trees.
plot	A small piece of land on which fruit, flowers or vegetables are grown.

patch

24 girl

lass   lassie

adolescent	A person soon to become an adult.
child	Someone older than a baby but not yet grown up.
juvenile	A person not yet an adult in the eyes of the law.
minor	A person below the age of 18.
schoolgirl	A girl still at school.
tomboy	A young girl who is rough and boylike in her behaviour.

damsel   wench

25 help

aid   assistance   support

comfort	Encouragement and sympathy especially in sorrow.
protection	Defence from harm.

reinforcement	The addition of strength.
relief	The removal or lessening of anxiety or pain.
rescue	The act of saving from danger.
service	

26 horse

cart-horse	A sturdy horse used for pulling carts.
colt	A young male horse.
filly	A young female horse.
foal	A new-born horse.
hunter	A strong horse used for cross-country riding.
mare	A fully-grown female horse.
mount	A horse ready for riding.
pony	A small fully grown horse.
racehorse	A horse used for racing.
stallion	A fully grown male horse.
thoroughbred	A horse bred from good ancestors.
steed	

27 house

bungalow	A house with only one floor level.
castle	An ancient fortress building.
cottage	A small house.
detached house	A house standing on its own.
flat	A set of rooms forming a complete home on one floor of a larger building.
hall	A large private house.
lodge	A small house at the entrance to a park or to the grounds of a mansion.
maisonette	(a) A self-contained dwelling on more than one floor, part of a larger building. (b) A small house.
manor	The home of the owner of an estate.
mansion	A large imposing residence.
palace	A large and splendid house, usually the home of a monarch, bishop or nobleman.
prefab	A house ready-made from assembled units.

semi-detached house	A house attached on one side to another dwelling.
shack	A roughly-built house.
terraced house	A house built as one of many in a continuous row.

bothy   chalet   manse   rectory   vicarage

28 island

isle

atoll	A ring-shaped coral island.
islet	A small island.

29 job

employment   occupation   post   situation   work

assignment	A task given to somebody.
chore	An unenjoyable job.
errand	A task entrusted to a messenger.
mission	A goal or object to be achieved.
profession	An occupation needing several years of study.
task	A hard piece of work which must be done.
trade	A skilled manual job.

calling   pursuit   vocation

30 land

continent	A very large unbroken area of land usually containing several countries.
country	(a) A land with well-marked boundaries and a name, inhabited by one nation.
	(b) Land away from the town.
district	A small area or locality.
island	A piece of land surrounded by water.
mainland	The larger part of a continent or country, apart from islands nearby.
parish	The area served by a church.

| province | A large area of a country considered as a whole. |
| region | An area of land with common features. |

county   estate   state   territory

31 light

brilliance	An intense brightness.
daylight	The light of day.
flare	A bright blaze of light sometimes used as a signal or target-marker.
flash	A sudden short burst of light.
glare	A fierce, steady bright light.
glow	A steady light.
moonlight	The light from the moon.
radiance	A light shining in bright rays.
sunlight	The light from the sun.
sunshine	As for Sunlight

dazzle   glimmer   glitter   gloss   illumination   phosphorescence

32 lot

abundance	A plentiful supply over and above what is necessary.
host	A very large crowd or army.
multitude	A great number, especially people.
profusion	A very great amount.

33 love

affection   fondness

devotion	A deep love.
friendship	A feeling of liking between friends.
liking	A feeling of attraction.
passion	A strong, sometimes uncontrolled, love.
regard	A feeling of kindly respect.
tenderness	A kind and sympathetic feeling.

34 meal

banquet	A magnificent meal eaten on a special occasion.
barbecue	An outdoor meal roasted or smoked over a special fire.
feast	A joyful meal eaten on a special occasion.
picnic	An outdoor meal using food previously packed.
snack	A light meal.
spread	An abundant meal of many courses or dishes.
repast	

35 money

cash   coinage   currency   notes   paper money.

bullion	Gold or silver bars.
finance	The money available to a nation, company or individual.
funds	Any cash one may have.
riches	A plentiful supply of money or valuables.
wealth	As for Riches.

36 mountain

hill	An area of raised ground smaller than a mountain.
ridge	The long narrow top or crest of land.
tor	An isolated mass of rock forming a peak.
highland *plateau*	

37 noise

sound

call	A cry or shout.
creak	A cracked grating sound.
cry	(a) A loud sound expressing emotion.
	(b) The call of an animal or bird.
howl	A long, loud, wavering cry.
murmur	A low, indistinct, drawn-out sound.

scream	A high-pitched cry.
screech	A long, harsh, piercing sound.
shriek	A high-pitched cry.
tap	The sound of a light blow.

roar   wail   whimper   whine

38 people

folk

brotherhood	A close group who share an interest or aim.
clan	A group of related families.
humanity	All men, women and children.
mankind	As for Humanity.
nation	The people of one country.
persons	Individual people.
population	All those persons living in a particular area.
society	A number of people, forming a group, having the same interests or purpose.
tribe	A group of people under a chief and sharing the same customs and beliefs.

community   public   race

39 picture

representation

cartoon	(a) A comic drawing.
	(b) A sketch for a later piece of work.
collage	A picture made by sticking many different things to a surface.
diagram	A line-drawing explaining something,
drawing	A picture made in crayon, pen and ink or pencil.
fresco	A picture painted on the plaster of a wall.
illustration	A picture showing a scene in a book or play.
landscape	A picture of town or countryside.
mosaic	A picture made up of small coloured pieces of the same material held closely together.

mural	A picture painted on a wall.
old master	A picture painted by a great artist of the past.
photograph	A picture produced by a camera.
portrait	A picture of a person.
poster	A picture advertising some product or event.
print	A reproduction of an original picture.
silhouette	A picture in profile done in a dark colour against a light background.
sketch	A rough draft for a picture.

40 price

charge   cost

estimate	A forecast of a price.
fare	The cost of travel.
fee	The sum paid to a professional person for service or advice.
quotation	A statement naming a price or estimate.
retail price	The price at which something is sold to the public.
tariff	A list of prices and charges.
value	The money someone would expect to pay for something.
wholesale price	The price charged by the maker to the shopkeeper or retailer.

rate

41 rain

cloudburst	A sharp downfall of very heavy rain likely to cause flooding.
deluge	A long very heavy rainfall usually causing flooding.
downpour	A short heavy fall of rain.
drizzle	Very fine rain.
monsoon	Very heavy steady rain during the wet season in some tropical countries.
Scotch mist	Fine drizzling rain.
scud	A shower driven by wind.
thunderstorm	Heavy rain with thunder and lightning.

42 **rest**

remainder	That which is left.
remnant	The remaining part or parts.
residue	As for Remainder.
surplus	An amount more than is necessary.

43 **road**

alley	A narrow passage between buildings.
avenue	A wide street often bordered by trees.
blind alley	An alley closed at one end.
by-pass	A road built for fast traffic to avoid a town.
by-road	A side road with little traffic.
by-way	A small road not often used.
cul-de-sac	A passage or road closed at one end.
drive	A private approach to a large building.
esplanade	A level promenade, especially along the seafront of a resort.
highway	A main road.
lane	A narrow country road.
motorway	A highway with many lanes, controlled by special laws, built for fast-moving traffic.
path	A pedestrian way.
route	A course or road chosen in travelling.
street	A road lined with buildings.
track	A rough way or path.
trunk road	A major road connecting large towns.

by-path   causeway

44 **sea**

briny   main

deep	(a) A deep part of the sea or ocean.
	(b) Any part of the sea very far from land.
ocean	A widespread area of sea.

high seas

45 ship

craft   vessel
aircraft-carrier   clipper   destroyer   frigate   liner   man-of-war
submarine   tanker

46 shop

bazaar	(a) An Eastern market.
	(b) A short sale of goods to raise money.
department store	A large shop selling many types of goods.
kiosk	A small light structure for the sale of newspapers, sweets, cigarettes, etc.
market	An open space or public building where goods are sold.
mart	As for Market.
self-service store	A shop in which customers serve themselves.
stall	A table or stand displaying goods for sale.
store	A large shop usually selling many different kinds of goods.
supermarket	A large self-service store selling various foods and household articles.
emporium	

47 shore

beach	The low-lying land at the water's edge.
coast	A stretch of land bordering the sea or a large area of water.
seashore	The beach at the sea's edge.
strand foreshore	

48 sleep

catnap	A short light sleep often taken sitting down.
doze	A light sleep.
forty winks	A short sleep.
hibernation	A natural sleep of some animals throughout the winter.
nap	As for Forty winks.
siesta	A midday sleep taken in hot countries.
snooze	As for Doze.
slumber	

49 story

tale

account	A connected story of events.
autobiography	A person's life story written by himself.
biography	A person's life story written by somebody else.
chronicle	A record of events usually in strict order of time.
description	An account setting out a picture in words.
diary	A day-to-day record of events.
fable	A short story which teaches a lesson.
fairy-tale	A tale of magical events and fairies.
folk-tale	A story passed down by word of mouth.
history	A record of past events showing their special importance.
legend	A story of gods or heroes once handed down by word of mouth but thought to have some truth.
memoirs	A book based on a person's memories.
novel	A story about imaginary people or events.
parable	A short story meant to teach a lesson about life.
romance	A pleasant imaginary love story.
saga	A long account of heroes and gods.
serial	A story told in several parts.
statement	A simple bare account.
thriller	An exciting story dealing with crime, detection, mysteries, etc.
yarn	A spun-out story often hard to believe and usually told aloud.

anecdote   fantasy   myth   narrative   report   travelogue

50 teacher

instructor   master   mistress

coach	One who prepares a person for an examination or sport.
governess	A lady who teaches young children in their home.
guru	A Hindu teacher of meditation or religious wisdom.
headmaster	The principal master of a school.
headmistress	The principal mistress of a school.
lecturer	One who delivers talks especially in a college or university.
principal	Head of a college or school etc.
professor	A teacher of the highest rank in a university department.

tutor	A teacher who gives lessons to one person or a very small group.

51 thief

bandit	An armed robber.
blackmailer	Someone who demands money by threatening to give away unpleasant secrets.
brigand	As for Bandit.
burglar	One who forces an entry into a house in order to steal.
embezzler	Someone who dishonestly uses money entrusted to him.
footpad	A highwayman who steals on foot.
highwayman	An armed horseman who robs travellers.
pickpocket	A person who steals from people's pockets.
pilferer	Someone who steals in small amounts.
pirate	Someone engaged in robbery on the high seas.
poacher	A person who catches fish or game without permission.
robber	One who takes goods or money.
shoplifter	Someone who deliberately takes things from a shop without paying.
swindler	One who cheats or defrauds.

kidnapper   kleptomaniac

52 top

apex   crown

brow	The top edge of a steep cliff or hill.
crest	The topmost point or edge.
peak	A pointed mountain top.
pinnacle	The highest pointed part of a mountain or building.
summit	The highest place.

zenith

53 war

civil war	A war between citizens of the same state or country.
crusade	A war for religious purposes.

guerrilla war	Irregular warfare carried on by small armed bands.
hostilities	Any acts of war.
total war	A war in which the whole population is attacked.

Armageddon   campaign   jihad

54 wood

brake	A clump of small bushes.
coppice	A wood of small trees cut from time to time.
copse	As for Coppice.
forest	An extensive area of land covered with trees.
grove	A group of trees.
plantation	A group of trees planted by man.
scrub	Brushwood, stunted trees or bushes.
spinney	A small wood or copse.
thicket	A dense growth of shrubs or trees.
woodland	Wooded country.

55 zoo

aquarium	A building containing a collection of glass-sided tanks for fish and water animals.
aviary	A large cage for keeping birds.
game park	A park where animals are kept and exhibited in the open.
menagerie	A collection of animals exhibited in captivity.
vivarium	A place for keeping live animals so that they may be easily observed.

Adjectives

56 big

enormous	Very much larger than usual.
fat	Oversized, sometimes due to over-eating.
gigantic	As big as a giant.
huge	As for Enormous.
hulking	Big and clumsy.
immense	As for Enormous.
massive	Large, heavy and impressive.
spacious	Having much space.
vast	Covering enormous space.

ample   bulky   colossal   considerable   elephantine   extensive   great king-sized   large   mammoth   mountainous   stout

57 boring

dull	Lacking variety or interest.
monotonous	Without any change.
tedious	Long and wearying.
tiresome	Wearying and irritating.
uninteresting	Arousing no interest.

humdrum   irksome   protracted   wearisome

58 brave

adventurous	Fond of dangerous, daring or exciting enterprises.
bold	Displaying daring and vigour.
courageous	Not affected by fear.
daring	Eager to face risk.
fearless	As for Courageous.
gallant	Courteous and protective.
heroic	So brave as to be admired by everyone.

enterprising   intrepid   resolute   stout-hearted   valiant

59 broken

burst	Shattered or split, usually by pressure from within.
destroyed	Broken, ruined.
shattered	Broken into pieces.

smashed	Broken into very small pieces.
split	Separated, broken apart.

cracked   fractured   splintered   spoiled

60 clean

bright	Unclouded and clear.
polished	Smooth and glossy.
shiny	Bright and luminous.
spotless	Perfectly clean.
stainless	Without dirty marks.
washed	Cleaned by water or other liquid.

undefiled   untainted

61 clever

brainy

able	Having the power or skill to do something.
astute	Keen, sharp-witted.
bright	Lively, quick to learn.
brilliant	Capable of a high performance.
capable	Able to handle most situations.
gifted	Born with great ability.
intelligent	Capable of reasoning.
skilful	Able to perform very well.
skilled	Thoroughly able.
smart	Sharply alert.
talented	Possessing high ability.
wise	Able to use experience and knowledge of many things well.

acute   competent   discerning   expert   shrewd

62 cold

chilly	Slightly but unpleasantly cold.
cool	Not very warm.
freezing	Cold enough to turn water into ice.
frosty	Nearly freezing.
frozen	So cold that water has been turned to ice.

icy	Cold as ice.
raw	Cold, damp and bleak.
shivery	Cold enough to make people shiver.
wintry	Cold, stormy and icy as in winter.

arctic   blistering   penetrating

63 dangerous

perilous

chancy	Uncertain, trusting to luck.
hazardous	Involving some risk.
menacing	As for Threatening.
risky	With the possible chance of injury or failure.
threatening	Suggesting that something harmful may happen.
treacherous	Safe-looking but dangerous.

ill-omened   ominous

64 dark

dim	Not completely dark.
dismal	Dark in a depressing way.
dull	Lacking clearness and vividness.
gloomy	With very little light.
murky	Shadowy and dingy.
obscure	Difficult to see.
shady	In shadow, out of the sun.
sombre	Gloomy, lacking in colour.
unlit	Without light.

opaque   overcast   sunless

65 dead

lifeless

extinct	Without further possibility of life.
inanimate	Without life.

deceased   defunct   demised   late   moribund

66 deep

bottomless	Having no bottom or end.

fathomless   *profound*   *unplumbed*

67 dirty

soiled   unclean

bedraggled	Soiled and wet.
dingy	Shabby and dull-looking, tinged with dirt.
dusty	Covered in dust.
filthy	In a very dirty condition.
foul	So dirty as to be smelly and offensive.
grimy	Having ingrained dirt.
messy	Dirty and untidy.
mucky	Extremely dirty.
muddy	Covered with mud or very wet earth.
slovenly	Careless and dirty in appearance.
smoky	Darkened by smoke.
sooty	Marked by soot.
stained	Marked by stains.
tarnished	Dirtied by exposure to the air, thereby losing gloss.

squalid

68 dry

arid	Very dry and lifeless.
crisp	Dry and easily broken.
dehydrated	Having no water content.
parched	In a waterless condition, dried up with the heat.
thirsty	Strongly desiring a drink.

desiccated   *waterless*

69 easy

simple

convenient	Handy and suitable.
effortless	Seemingly without effort.

facile   Easily, almost carelessly done.
painless   Causing no pain.
undemanding   Making no demands of effort, time or thought.
manageable   yielding

70 empty

bare

blank   (a) Unmarked, as a page in a book.
                   (b) Expressionless, as a person's face.
hollow   Having the inside empty.
uninhabited   With no one living there, as of countries, islands, etc.
unoccupied   As for Uninhabited, but of houses.
vacant   Not occupied, usually for a long time.
deserted   void

71 exciting

arresting   striking

dramatic   Striking and impressive as in a film or play.
gripping   Strongly holding interest.
interesting   Arousing interest.
sensational   Causing great excitement.
stimulating   Causing lively interest.
fascinating   thrilling

72 famous

celebrated   Well-known and honoured.
immortal   Known throughout all ages past and future.
infamous   Of bad reputation.
notable   Worth notice.
noted   As for Celebrated.
notorious   Widely known for evil deeds.
renowned   Well-known.
distinguished   eminent   reputable

73 **fast**

rapid   swift

hasty	Too quick for carefulness.
hurried	As for Hasty.
lively	Moving with vigour and energy.
prompt	Done quickly or at once.
quick	Fast for a short time.
speedy	Rapid and nimble.
fleet nimble	

74 **fat**

buxom	Plump in an attractive way.
chubby	Round-faced with plump cheeks.
heavy	Of great weight.
obese	Extremely overweight.
overweight	Heavier than one should be.
plump	Pleasantly fat.
corpulent portly	*pot-bellied stout*

75 **full**

brimful	Full to the top edge.
bulging	Swelling outwards.
overflowing	Running over the edge or lip.
saturated	Containing as much liquid as can be absorbed.
topped up	Filled up to the top.
brimming crammed replete	

76 **happy**

glad   joyful   joyous

blissful	Full of supreme happiness.
contented	Well pleased.
delighted	Intensely happy.

elated		In high spirits.
merry		Full of mirth.
satisfied		Wanting nothing more.
cheerful	*content*	*optimistic* *pleased*

77 hard

difficult

arduous		Calling for great effort.
demanding		Calling for effort, strength or intelligence.
formidable	*laborious*	*onerous*

78 hot

oppressive	Sultry, heavy and exhaustingly hot.
red-hot	Heated to glowing.
scalding	Hot enough as a liquid to cause blisters.
sultry	Very hot without much air.
sweltering	Oppressively hot, causing sweating.
torrid	So hot as to dry up and scorch.

blistering   burning   feverish   scorching   sizzling   stifling   tropical

79 hungry

famished	Very hungry.
peckish	Slightly hungry.
ravenous	Extremely hungry.
starving	Likely to die of hunger.

80 ill

ailing   unwell

bedridden	Unable to move from bed because of illness.
feverish	Ill with a high temperature.
indisposed	Unable to behave freely because of illness.

mortally ill	Certain to die from an incurable illness.
seedy	A little unwell.
decrepit poorly sick	

81 **last**

ultimate

concluding	Bringing to an end.
extreme	At the furthest limit.
final	Coming at the end.
hindmost	At the end of a line.
rear terminal	

82 **late**

tardy

behindhand	Late with some task or appointment.
belated	Overdue, behind time.
last-minute	At the latest possible time.
overdue	Later than the appointed time.
dilatory unpunctual	

83 **lazy**

indolent

idle	Inactive, avoiding effort.
slothful	Lazy and unwilling to make an effort.
slack	

84 **light** (i)

bright	Having much light.
brilliant	Sparkling and dazzling.
fiery	Giving off a burning glow.
glistening	Looking wet and shiny.

glittering	Shining brightly at rapid intervals.
luminous	Giving off light.
shiny	Bright and luminous.
sparkling	Shining brightly but in small flashes.

dazzling   incandescent   radiant

85 light (ii)

lightweight   featherweight

| feathery | Almost without weight. |
| portable | Able to be carried. |

airy   buoyant   weightless

86 little

small

microscopic	Too small to be seen except through a microscope.
minute	Very tiny.
pocket-sized	Small enough to fit into a pocket.
tiny	Very small.
wee	As for Tiny.

dwarf   midget   miniature   pint-sized

87 more

additional   extra   further   increased

88 near

neighbouring   nearby   next

adjoining	Attached.
approaching	Coming close to.
local	In the neighbouring area.

adjacent   handy

89 new

brand-new	Fresh from the manufacturer.
fresh	Recently produced or made.
modern	Up-to-date.
novel	Not known before.
original	Made or expressed for the first time.
recent	In the near past.
up-to-date	Up to the latest standards.

new-fangled

90 nice

agreeable	Pleasant and comfortable.
amusing	Pleasantly entertaining.
charming	Delightful and attractive.
comfortable	Offering pleasant conditions of life.
delightful	Giving great pleasure.
enjoyable	Giving enjoyment.
pleasant	Giving pleasure.
pleasing	As for Pleasant.
refreshing	Pleasantly different or new.
restful	Giving an impression of peace and quiet.
satisfying	Completely fulfilling needs or wishes.

attractive   cheering   glorious   gratifying

91 old

aged   elderly

ancient	Of very great age.
antique	Valued for age (of furniture, etc.).
historical	Of interest because of its place in the past.
medieval	Concerned with the period of the Middle Ages.
prehistoric	Before recorded history.
senile	So old as to be weak in mind and body.
venerable	Respected and honoured because of age.

antiquated   mythological   old-fashioned   traditional

92 open

accessible	Easy to get at or into.
ajar	Only just open.
gaping	Wide open.
unfenced	Without a fence.
yawning	

93 poor

bankrupt	Unable to meet one's debts.
broke	Without money, usually for a short time only.
destitute	Completely without money or property.
hard up	Short of money.
in want	In need of money.
needy	Without goods or money necessary for life.
penniless	Without money.
poverty-stricken	Very poor.
beggarly impecunious	

94 pretty

beautiful	Very attractive to look at.
fair	Of clear and bright appearance.
lovely	Of attractive appearance.
neat	Set out in a tidy way.
ornamental	Decorated to create a pleasing appearance.
picturesque	Of striking and colourful appearance.
splendid	Magnificent or glorious.
stylish	Smartly in fashion.
elegant exquisite graceful	

95 quiet

hushed	Made silent.
noiseless	Without noise.
silent	Without sound.
tranquil	Peaceful and pleasant.
muted stifled	

96 ready (i)

mature	Fully developed or ripe.
prepared	Ready for use.
ripe	Grown and suitable for use.

97 ready (ii)

alert	In readiness, on the look-out.
prepared	Ready for action.
expectant	

98 rich

opulent   wealthy

affluent	Well supplied with possessions and money.
flush moneyed	

99 right

accurate	Strictly correct in all details.
correct	Without fault or mistake.
exact	Accurate in every detail.
precise	As for Exact.
true	In agreement with the facts.
unerring	

100 sad

miserable   sorrowful   unhappy

dejected	Cast down in spirits.
depressed	In low spirits.
disappointed	With one's hopes and expectations not realized.
discontented	Dissatisfied and unhappy.
gloomy	As for Depressed.
grief-stricken	In deep distress.
dismal dispirited	*dreary joyless lugubrious sombre*

101 safe

immune	Secure from any danger.
protected	Defended from harm.
secure	Free from danger, fear or attack.
sheltered	Safe from weather or danger.
shielded	Given protection by some sort of screen.

impregnable   invulnerable   unassailable

102 slow

deliberate	After careful thought.
gradual	Happening steadily a small stage at a time.
leisurely	Calm and without haste.
sluggish	Moving in a slow lazy manner.
unhurried	Without any appearance of urgency.

dilatory   snail-like   tortoise-like

103 soft

downy

cushiony	Giving soft support.
fleecy	Soft and woolly.
spongy	Soft and absorbent.

flabby   limp   pliable

104 strong

powerful

hardy	Able to resist hardships.
irresistible	Overpowering.
mighty	Of great strength and power.
stalwart	Loyal and courageous in the face of attacks.
sturdy	Strong and reliable under pressure.
tough	Firm and hardy.

herculean   overwhelming

105 thin

bony	Extremely thin so that the bones show.
gaunt	Thin and hungry looking.
lean	Without spare fat.
meagre	As for Lean.
spare	As for Lean.
wiry	Thin but tough and sinewy.

lanky   scrawny   skinny   slender   slim   willowy

106 tight

compressed	Packed closely together.
jammed	Pressed tightly against.
stuck	Unable to move in any direction.
wedged	Immovably held in position.

107 ugly

ghastly	Hideously frightening.
grisly	Horribly unpleasant.
gruesome	As for Grisly.
hideous	Very ugly.
horrible	Causing a feeling of disgust.
monstrous	Unnaturally large and shocking.
repulsive	As for Horrible.
unsightly	Unpleasant to look at.

forbidding   mis-shapen   repellent   shocking

108 warm

close	Warm and airless.
lukewarm	Neither hot nor cold.
mild	Not cold.
muggy	Warm and damp.
sunny	Warmed by the sun.
tepid	Only slightly warm.

109 weak

feeble	Very weak.
frail	Very weak and fragile.
fragile	Easy broken.
infirm	Very open to illness or accident.
decrepit	

110 wet

damp	Only very slightly wet.
drenched	Very wet.
dripping	Wet with drips falling off.
flooded	Covered with water.
moist	As for Damp.
soaked	Wet through and through.
waterlogged	So full of water as hardly to float.
watery	Containing water.
saturated *sodden*	

111 wide

broad	Of great size across.
expansive	Of great size and extent.
extensive	Spreading over a wide range.
spacious	As for Expansive.
wide-ranging	As for Extensive.
ample	

112 young

youthful

adolescent	Between childhood and adulthood.
boyish	Like a boy.
childlike	Like a child.
girlish	Like a young girl.
immature	Not fully developed, lacking sense or wisdom.
teenage	Of ages 13–19.
juvenile	

Verbs

113 answer

reply   respond

acknowledge	(a) To admit that something is true or has happened.
	(b) To announce the receipt of something.
echo	To repeat at once.
retort	To answer back angrily or sharply.
write back	To answer by letter.

114 ask

beg	To ask earnestly (for help of some kind).
demand	To request with authority.
enquire	To ask for information.
entreat	To ask seriously and earnestly.
implore	As for Entreat but in fear of refusal.
inquire	As for Enquire.
invite	To ask, as to a party, game or house.

appeal   beseech   plead   request

115 beat

defeat	To overcome after a struggle.
overcome	To reach victory.
overthrow	To remove from a position of power by force.

conquer   crush   trounce

116 begin

commence   start

found	To lay a base for growth.
launch	To set moving for the first time, sometimes with some ceremony.
originate	To make for the first time.

establish   inaugurate   initiate   institute

117 break

fracture   snap

burst	To break apart violently from within.
crack	To split without destroying the original form.
damage	To injure or harm.
demolish	To pull or knock down into ruins.
destroy	To spoil beyond repair or further use.
shatter	To break suddenly into many pieces.
smash	To break into pieces by a heavy blow or blows.
split	To force or tear apart, especially lengthways.

crumble   rend

118 build

construct	To make by putting together.
create	To make something that has not existed before.
erect	To set upright, as with a building.

form

119 burn

brand	To mark by the pressure of hot metal.
char	To blacken with heat.
cremate	To burn to ashes, usually a dead body.
gut	To burn out the inside of a building.
scald	To burn skin and flesh by contact with hot liquid or vapour.
scorch	To burn the outside of.
singe	To burn the outside slightly.

consume

120 buy

purchase

barter	To trade by exchange, using goods rather than money.
pay for	To give money in return for goods or services.
swap	To exchange.
swop	As for Swap.

121 carry

bear

convey	To take from one place to another.
ferry	To carry passengers or goods across water.
ship	To transport or send by ship.
transport	To take from one place to another.

bring   fetch   take

122 catch

ambush	To wait in hiding and take by surprise.
capture	To take and keep by force.
hook	To catch or fasten with a hook.
net	To trap by catching in a net.
seize	To take by force.
snare	To catch in a trap using a noose.
trap	To capture by a hidden device or trick.

decoy   ensnare   entrap   lure   waylay

123 chase

follow	To pursue.
hound	To pursue ruthlessly.
hunt	To pursue in order to capture or kill.
pursue	To follow someone or something in order to catch up or overtake.
search for	To look for in many places.
seek	As for Search for.
shadow	To follow closely without being seen.
stalk	To hunt, keeping out of sight.
track	To hunt by following the signs left by an animal or person.
trail	As for Track.

dog   tag   tail

124 choose

elect	To choose someone from a group, usually by voting.
pick	To choose from a selection.
select	To pick out by some standard.
adopt	*vote for*

125 clean

bath	To wash a person or animal in a bath.
cleanse	To make clean or pure.
dry-clean	To clean with chemicals rather than water.
launder	To wash and iron linen and clothes.
mop	To clean or wipe with a mop.
purify	To make free of unwanted substances.
rinse	To wash out with water.
scour	To clean by rubbing with some rough surface or powder.
scrub	To rub vigorously with brush, soap and water.
shampoo	To wash by rubbing with a soap-like liquid.
sponge	To clean or wipe with a sponge.
spring-clean	To clean a room or house with extra thoroughness, usually after winter.
wash	To clean with soap and water.

126 close

shut

bolt	To fasten, with a sliding rod. (For example: a door or window.)
lock	To close using a lock and key.
seal	To shut up and close, as with an envelope.
secure	To close and make safe.
slam	To shut violently and noisily.

127 copy

ape	To imitate, especially mockingly.
duplicate	To make one or more exact copies.

echo	To repeat sounds at once.
forge	To copy for a criminal purpose.
imitate	To copy very closely.
mirror	To reflect, as in a mirror.
repeat	To do or say something again.
reproduce	To repeat, copying exactly.
trace	To draw on a thin covering sheet following lines seen on a picture beneath.

emulate   impersonate   mimic

128 cry

shed tears   weep

blubber	To weep more noisily than necessary.
howl	To weep with drawn-out cries of rage or pain.
sob	To weep in a gasping way.
wail	To weep with long cries of grief.
whimper	To cry feebly.

129 cut

chop	To cut, usually by striking with an axe or knife.
fell	To cut down and bring to the ground.
gash	To make a long deep cut.
graze	To scrape or scratch a surface or skin.
hack	To cut or chop roughly, especially with an axe.
hew	To cut down or fell with an axe.
saw	To cut using a tool with a toothed edge.
sever	To separate by cutting.
skin	To remove the outer coat or skin by cutting and pulling.
slash	To make long cuts by striking fiercely.
slice	To cut into thin strips.
slit	To split by making a long clean cut or tear.

cleave   lacerate   mangle   sunder

130 dig

excavate	(a) To dig out and leave a hole.
	(b) To dig in order to find remains.
hoe	To remove weeds from between plants by light digging.
hollow	To dig a hole by scooping out.
plough	To turn over soil with a plough.
shovel	To shift earth, sand or coal etc., using a large scoop.
tunnel	To dig through earth and rock to form a passage.

burrow   mine

131 drink

gulp	(a) To swallow noisily or greedily.
	(b) To swallow with difficulty.
guzzle	To swallow greedily in large quantities.
sip	To drink in small amounts.
suck	To draw into the mouth using lips and lungs.
swallow	To pass from the mouth into the stomach.
swig	To drink in large amounts.
swill	To drink greedily.
taste	To try the flavour of.
toast	To drink to the health or success of someone.

quaff   sup   tipple

132 dry

air	To remove the last possible dampness by placing in warm air.
dehydrate	To remove all water, as with dried vegetables.
drain	To cause water to run away.
evaporate	To remove water by heating.
hang out	To hang up to dry in the sun or wind.

133 eat

feed

banquet	To feast in a magnificent style on a special occasion.
dine	To eat dinner at midday or in the evening.

feast	To eat in a joyful way on a special occasion.
gobble	To swallow in lumps.
gorge	To eat greedily until no more can be eaten.
nibble	To eat in very small bites.
swallow	To pass from the mouth into the stomach.
taste	To try the flavour of.
tuck in	To eat hungrily.

bolt   devour   guzzle

134 enjoy

like	To be fond of or attracted to.
relish	To have a keen enjoyment in.
revel in	To take intense pleasure in.

bask in   wallow in

135 fall

drop

cascade	To fall like a waterfall.
collapse	To fall down suddenly.
descend	To go down.
plummet	To fall violently straight down.
plunge	To jump downwards (into or through).
sink	To move down slowly, usually through water.
slump	To fall suddenly and helplessly.
subside	To settle down or sink slowly.
tumble	To fall headlong.

come a cropper   topple

136 farm

breed	To raise a particular kind of animal for certain qualities.
cultivate	(a) To make fertile and productive for growing crops.
	(b) To grow crops.
dig	To turn over soil.
grow	To produce plants or crops.

harvest	To gather fully grown crops.
raise	To grow something, usually crops or animals.
ranch	To work a large area with machines, cattle or horses.
reap	To cut the crops of grain.
rear	To breed and look after during growth.
sow	To plant seeds.
till	As for Cultivate (a).

137 find

chance on	To find by accident.
discover	To find out for the first time.
encounter	To meet with or come across.
find out	To discover after an enquiry.
locate	To find the exact position of.
realize	To become aware of and understand clearly.
ferret out *unearth*	

138 fix

correct   put right   set right

amend	To put right a mistake by altering.
cure	To restore to health.
mend	To restore to good shape and order.
repair	As for Mend.
restore	To bring back to former condition.

139 fly

ascend	To go up.
become airborne	To leave the ground at the start of a flight.
descend	To go down.
dive	To swoop steeply.
glide	To fly, using air currents for power.
hover	To stay fairly still in the sky by use of wings.
rise	To move upwards.
sail	As for Glide.

soar	(a) To fly at a great height.
	(b) To fly without moving wings.
swoop	To fly rapidly downwards, usually in attack.

140 **follow** (i) (See Chase)

141 **follow** (ii)

come after   come next   ensue   go next

| go after | To fill in the place behind. |
| succeed | To come next after and take the place of. |

142 **get**

achieve	To reach or win after much effort.
acquire	To gain possession of.
earn	To receive as payment for work.
gain	(a) To obtain by effort.
	(b) To increase (possessions).
obtain	As for Acquire.
procure	To obtain after careful thought and effort.
win	To gain something as a prize in a contest.

annex   attain   gather   reach   secure

143 **give**

award	To give as a reward for effort.
bestow	To give as a sign of favour.
confer	As for Bestow.
contribute	(a) To make a gift in support of something.
	(b) To send an article for publication.
donate	To make a gift usually of money in support of a cause.
grant	To give in response to a request.
leave	To arrange a payment to be made after one's death.

present   To give on a special occasion.
provide   To supply for use.
render   To hand over, usually as a form of duty.
accord   bequeath   subscribe

144 go

abscond   To run away and hide from authority.
bolt   To run away suddenly without warning.
depart   To leave, usually for a journey.
escape   To free oneself from danger.
flee   To run away from a threat of danger.
leave   To go away from a place.
move   To leave, taking one's goods to another place.
remove   As for Move.
elope

145 hate

detest   loathe

dislike   To feel an objection towards.
abhor   abominate

146 have

keep   To remain in possession of something.
occupy   To hold or live in a place.
own   To have by right.
possess   As for Own.
retain   To continue to have.
corner   monopolize

147 hear

eavesdrop   To listen secretly to a private conversation.
overhear   To hear a conversation by accident.
monitor

148 **help**

aid   assist

accommodate	To supply something needed, especially board and lodging.
advise	To suggest what to do.
comfort	To encourage and offer support.
counsel	To advise and offer an opinion.
oblige	To do a service as a favour.
reinforce	To give extra help or strength.
stand by	To remain loyal to.
support	To provide for the needs of.
sustain	As for Support.

149 **hide**

conceal

cover up	(a) To hide something by covering it.
	(b) To conceal or disguise, especially a fact.
disguise	To change in appearance in order to deceive.
mask	To place a covering over, usually the face.
screen	To prevent from being seen.
secrete	To keep in a secret place.
suppress	To keep back so that no-one else will know.
camouflage	

150 **hit**

strike

batter	To strike repeatedly with heavy blows.
beat	To strike repeatedly with force.
flog	To hit repeatedly with a whip or stick.
knock	To give a short sharp blow.
lash	To hit with a cord attached to a handle.
punch	To hit with the fist.
rap	To hit with a sudden quick blow.
scourge	To strike repeatedly with a knotted cord.
slap	To hit with the open hand.

smack	As for Slap.
spank	To hit with the open hand, especially on the bottom.
tap	To strike lightly.
thrash	As for Flog.
thump	To strike with a dull blow.
whip	As for Lash.

belabour   buffet   dab   flail   flay   hammer   pummel

151 join

ally	To unite for a common purpose.
assemble	To put together from parts.
fit together	As for Assemble.
fuse	To melt together.
solder	To join two metal surfaces by melting a soft metal on them.
unite	To join together as one.
weld	To join metal surfaces by the use of intense heat.

dovetail   rivet

152 jump

bound	To spring upwards or forwards.
hop	To jump on one leg.
leap	To jump over, across or up in the air.
plunge	To jump quickly into something.
spring	To move suddenly and rapidly.
vault	To leap over, usually with the help of hand or pole.

caper   gambol

153 keep

hold	To keep possession of.
preserve	To keep in good condition.
put away	Put aside for future use.
retain	To hold in one's possession.
store	Put in a safe place.
withhold	To keep back and so refuse.

detain   imprison   secure

154 kill

put to death   slay

decimate	To destroy large numbers.
execute	To kill as a punishment, usually after a trial.
exterminate	To kill off all of a kind.
massacre	To kill in very large numbers.
murder	To kill a person after planning to do so.
sacrifice	To kill as an offering.
slaughter	(a) To kill very large numbers.
	(b) To kill animals for food.

155 know

grasp	To understand information fully.
realize	To become aware of and understand clearly.
recognize	To know from a previous meeting.
understand	To know the full meaning of.

comprehend   identify

156 love

appreciate	To realize the value or quality of someone or something.
care for	To have a liking for.
cherish	To value dearly.
hold dear	To have a great liking for.
like	To be fond of, to be attracted to.
prize	To value highly.
treasure	To think of and treat as very valuable.
value	To think highly of.

adore   idolize   worship

157 make

produce

build	To make by putting together.
compose	To make up poetry or music.

construct	As for Build.
create	To make something that has not existed before.
erect	To set upright as in a building.
invent	To make for the very first time.
manufacture	To make goods on a large scale, usually by machinery.

fashion   hew   shape

158 meet

assemble	To come together.
congregate	To gather together.

cluster   muster   throng

159 move

budge	To move a very short distance.
drive	To cause to move forwards or backwards under control.
eject	To throw or push something out.
fly	To move in the air under control.
propel	To drive along.
sail	To use the wind as power for movement.
shift	To change the position of something.

160 need

lack	To be without.
require	To depend on for success.
want	To be in need of.

161 open

open out   open up

break open	To open by force.
prise open	To force open with a lever.
uncork	To take the cork from.
unfold	To open out the folds.

162 pay

award	To give after considering merit.
compensate	To make up for loss or injury, usually by a payment of money.
refund	To give back money.
repay	To pay back.
reward	To offer something, sometimes money, for services.
tip	To give extra money for service.

recompense   reimburse

163 plant

grow	To plant and tend until fully grown.
sow	To set in a place suitable for growth.
transplant	To dig up from one place and plant elsewhere.

164 play

amuse oneself	To occupy oneself agreeably.
fool about	To play in a silly manner.
frolic	To leap about playfully.
have fun	To enjoy oneself.
romp	To play noisily.

frisk   gambol   revel   sport

165 put

deposit   put down   set down

lay	To put down, usually carefully.
place	To set down in a particular area.
position	To place on a particular spot.

166–169

166 rain

drizzle	To rain very finely.
mizzle	As for Drizzle.
pour	To rain heavily.
shower	To rain for a short time.
teem	To rain very heavily.

167 rest

lie down	To take a reclining position.
pause	To stop for a while.
relax	To stop straining.
repose	

168 rob

burgle	To enter secretly and steal.
embezzle	To steal for one's own use money entrusted to one's care.
hold up	To rob using weapon or threats.
loot	To seize unprotected goods in time of war or other disaster.
pilfer	To steal in small amounts.
pillage	To take away by force.
plunder	As for Pillage.
raid	To make a sudden attack in order to seize or destroy goods.
rifle	To search and steal.
rustle	To steal livestock.
steal	To take something from someone dishonestly and secretly.
blackmail kidnap poach thieve	

169 rub

buff	To polish using a special leather or felt.
chafe	To damage or irritate by rubbing.
file	To wear down using a rough metal strip.
grind	To wear down using a rough stone.
polish	To make smooth and glossy by rubbing.
smooth	To make a surface even.
wipe	To clean or dry by rubbing with a cloth.

170 run

charge	To rush violently against.
chase	To pursue in order to catch.
dash	To run a short distance suddenly and quickly.
flee	To try to escape by running away.
gallop	To run like a horse at full speed.
jog	To move along at a slow bouncing trot.
lope	To run strongly and smoothly in long strides.
scamper	To run quickly with short steps.
scurry	To run hurriedly with quick short steps.
sprint	To run at full speed over a short distance.
trot	To run along slowly.

171 save

protect	To guard from danger.
rescue	To set free from danger.
retrieve	To recover after losing.
salvage	To save from possible destruction.
extricate	

172 say

remark   speak   state   utter

affirm	To state strongly.
announce	To state publicly.
comment	To make remarks about a subject.
declare	As for Announce.
hint	To make a slight suggestion, usually indirectly.
mention	To speak or write about briefly.
preach	To make a public speech about religion.
rant	To talk stormily and noisily.
rave	To shout angrily and wildly as if mad.
recite	To repeat aloud usually from memory.
shout	To call out loudly.
snap	To make an angry sharp reply.
whisper	To speak without using the voice.
declaim	*lecture* *observe* *orate* *pronounce*

173 see

witness

examine	To study carefully.
gaze at	To look at steadily.
glance at	To take a quick look at.
glare at	To look at fiercely and angrily.
glimpse	To catch sight of for a short time.
inspect	To look closely into.
look at	As for Behold.
notice	To become aware of.
observe	To watch carefully.
perceive	As for Notice.
recognize	To know something again as already seen.
scrutinize	To examine closely.
stare at	To look at with fixed wide open eyes.
study	To look thoughtfully at.
view	To look over.

behold   consider   mark   note   regard   sight

174 send

broadcast	To send out a message over a wide area as by TV or radio.
consign	To send by special arrangement.
dispatch	To send off.
post	To send through the mail.
ship	To send off by ship.
transmit	To send a signal or message from one place to another.

175 shine

blaze	To shine strongly and brilliantly.
dazzle	To blind by a glaring light for a short time.
flash	To send out a sudden brief bright ray of light.
flicker	To burn unsteadily.
gleam	To shine out, not very brightly but steadily.
glitter	To shine brightly in small flashes.
glow	To send out a steady faint light.

sparkle	As for Glitter.
twinkle	To send out small rapid flashes of uneven brightness.
glare *glimmer* *scintillate*	

176 shout

bawl	To shout out in a harsh rough voice.
bellow	To shout loudly and angrily.
chant	To shout together as a crowd.
cheer	To make shouts of applause and encouragement.
clamour	To make a noise of opposition and complaint.
cry out	To make a loud cry.
exclaim	To cry out suddenly and loudly.
roar	To make a long, deep, continuous noise.
scream	To make a long shrill cry.
yell	To cry out loudly.

177 sing

croon	To sing softly and gently.
hum	To produce a low sound with the lips closed.
warble	To sing with a trembling effect.
chant *trill* *yodel*	

178 sit

| squat | To sit almost on the ground with the knees drawn up. |

179 sleep

doze	To sleep lightly.
drowse	To be half asleep.
hibernate	To sleep through the winter.
nod	To be nearly asleep.
nod off	To fall asleep.
snooze	To take a short sleep.
slumber	

180 stay

remain

endure	To remain firm despite difficultues.
last	To remain in spite of the passage of time.
stand	To remain firmly in one place.
stand fast	As for Stand.

abide   continue   tarry

181 stop (i)

cease   conclude   end   finish

182 stop (ii)

prevent

forbid	To order not to do.
impede	To hinder progress.
prohibit	To forbid, especially by law.

bar   deny   exclude   halt

183 take

clasp	To hold closely.
clutch	To reach out quickly in order to grasp.
fetch	To go for and bring.
grab	To seize quickly.
grasp	To seize firmly.
seize	To grasp suddenly.
snatch	To take away by sudden force.

abstract   appropriate   kidnap

184 talk

chat	To talk easily and casually.
converse	To talk with another person.
gossip	To chat about people or events.

mumble	To speak not very clearly.
murmur	To speak in a soft low voice.
whisper	To speak using breath only.

debate declaim dispute gabble harangue lecture prattle preach rant spout

185 teach

coach	To prepare someone for an examination or a contest.
educate	To instruct and develop the growth of a person.
instruct	To give knowledge to.
lecture	To deliver a prepared talk to an audience.
train	To instruct through practice.
tutor	To teach one person rather than a group.

cram enlighten

186 think

consider	To think something over.
contemplate	To view in one's mind.
daydream	To allow the mind to wander.
imagine	To form a picture or idea in one's mind.
ponder	To think something over carefully.
reflect	To think carefully about something.

meditate

187 throw

cast	To throw outwards, often aiming at something.
fling	To throw wildly but without careful aim.
heave	To lift and throw with great effort.
hurl	To throw very strongly.
pitch	To throw with care aiming to reach a definite target.
sling	To throw in a wild manner.
toss	To throw aside or upwards with a light quick action.

catapult launch put

188 touch

brush	To touch lightly in passing.
caress	To stroke fondly in a loving manner.
feel	To sense by touch.
graze	To touch or scrape lightly in passing.
handle	To touch or feel with the hands.
manipulate	To control or work by the hands.
press	To put pressure on, or push against.
rub	To move with pressure over a surface.
scrape	To rub or scratch with something rough or sharp.
tickle	To touch so as to cause laughter.
contact	

189 try

attempt	To make an effort.
endeavour	To try very hard against difficulty.
strive	To make great effort.
venture	

190 use

employ

consume	To use up by eating, drinking or burning.
expend	To use up.
exploit	To make use of unfairly.
operate	To be in control of something whilst it is in action.
utilize	To make use of.

191 wait

dawdle	To act or move slowly.
hang about	To linger or loiter.
kill time	To pass the time in a way that avoids boredom.
linger	To wait about, not wanting to leave.
loiter	To wait about, without a purpose.

queue	To wait one's turn in a line of people or vehicles.
stand by	To remain alert and waiting.

192 walk

hobble	To walk with shortened steps.
limp	To walk lamely.
march	To walk with regular rhythmic steps.
pace	To walk slowly with regular steps.
plod	To walk slowly and heavily.
shuffle	To walk with a dragging irregular walk.
stagger	To walk very unsteadily.
stride	To walk with long steps.
stroll	To walk at ease.
trudge	To walk slowly and with effort.
waddle	To walk with short steps swaying like a duck.

*amble   lurch   prowl   reel   rove   saunter   step   strut   swagger
toddle   totter*

193 want

crave	To want very much.
desire	To long for.
long for	As for Crave.
wish for	To feel a need for.

require

194 watch

look at

gaze at	To look steadily at.
observe	To watch carefully.
pay attention to	To take special notice of.

behold   view

195 **write** (i)

engrave	To cut lines into a hard surface.
inscribe	To write, carve or engrave on.
print	To make lettering on paper.
scrawl	To write in hasty, badly-formed writing.
scribble	As for Scrawl.

196 **write** (ii)

compose	To write, for the first time, poetry or music.
jot	To write information in short form.
note	As for Jot.
record	To put down in writing.

chronicle   report

Adverbs

197 afterwards

after   subsequently   then

later   At a time following.
thereafter

198 always

endlessly   eternally   everlastingly   evermore   permanently   perpetually
unceasingly

constantly   In a way that does not change.
continually   Over and over again.
continuously   Without a break.
incessantly   Without ceasing.
invariably   Continually the same.

199 carefully

cautiously   Taking great care not to make a mistake.
mindfully   Keeping something carefully in mind.
thoughtfully   As for Mindfully.
circumspectly   conscientiously   considerately   meticulously   warily

200 easily

effortlessly   simply

freely   Without any holding back or snags.
smoothly   As for Freely.

201 fast

quickly   rapidly   speedily   swiftly

hastily   Quickly, without proper care.
hurriedly   As for Hastily.

202 nicely

agreeably

delightfully	In a delightful way.
enjoyably	In an enjoyable way.
pleasingly	In a pleasing way.
satisfyingly	In a satisfying way.

203 now

at once   immediately   promptly

204 often

daily	Every day.
frequently	Many times.
repeatedly	Over and over again.

205 slowly

lingeringly   sluggishly

leisurely	Without haste.
unhurriedly	Without any hurry.

206 so

accordingly   consequently   therefore

207 suddenly

abruptly	In a sudden and unexpected way.
hastily	Quickly without proper case.
hurriedly	As for Hastily.
promptly	At once.
unexpectedly	In a surprising way.

208 **then**

afterwards   at that time   formerly   lately   once   presently   soon
tomorrow   yesterday

209 **too**

also

additionally	In addition to.
besides	As well as.
further	As for Additionally.
moreover	As for Additionally.

210 **very**

exceedingly	So as to surpass all others.
exceptionally	As an exception to a rule.
exquisitely	Far beyond expected standards.
extremely	So as to reach the limit.
quite	Just . . . enough.
remarkably	So as to be worthy of attention.
utterly	As for Extremely.
intensely	

Index

adj = adjective
adv = adverb
  n = noun

Words printed in **bold type** are key words
The past tenses of all verbs are given.

A

abhor   abhorred 145
abide   abode 180
able 61
abominate   abominated 145
abruptly 207
abscond   absconded 144
abstract   abstracted 183
abundance 32
accessible 92
accommodate   accommodated
    148
accord   accorded 143
accordingly 206
account 49
accurate 99
achieve   achieved 142
acknowledge   acknowledged 113
acquaintance 21
acquire   acquired 142
acute 61
additional 87
additionally 209
adjacent 88
adjoining 88
adolescent (n) (boy) 10
adolescent (n) (girl) 24
adolescent (adj) 112
adopt   adopted 124
adore   adored 156
adventurous 58
advise   advised 148
affection 33
affirm   affirmed 172
affluent 98
affray 19
after 197

afterwards 197
afterwards (then) 208
aged 91
agreeable 90
agreeably 202
aid (n) 25
aid   aided 148
ailing 80
air   aired 132
aircraft-carrier 45
airy 85
ajar   92
album 8
alert 97
all 1
alley 43
allied   *see* ally
allotment 23
ally (n) 21
ally   allied 151
also 209
always 198
amble   ambled 192
ambush   ambushed 122
amend   amended 138
ample (big) 56
ample (wide) 111
amphibian 2
amuse oneself   amused oneself
    164
amusing 90
ancient 91
anecdote 49
animal 2
annex   annexed 142
annihilate   annihilated 115
announce   announced 172
anorak 15

answer (n) 3
answer   answered 113
anthology 8
antiquated 91
antique 91
ape   aped 127
apex 52
appeal   appealed 114
appreciate   appreciated 156
approaching 88
appropriate   appropriated 183
aquarium 55
arctic 62
arduous 77
arid 68
Armageddon 53
armchair 13
arresting 71
ascend   ascended 139
ask   asked 114
assemble   assembled (join) 151
assemble   assembled (meet) 158
assignment 29
assist   assisted 148
assistance 25
associate 21
astute 61
ate   *see* **eat**
atlas 8
atoll 28
at once 203
attain   attained 142
attempt   attempted 189
at that time 208
attractive 90
audience 16
autobiography 49
automobile 12
avenue 43
aviary 55
award   awarded (give) 143
award   awarded (pay) 162

B
baby 4
bag 5
bairn 4
ball 6
bandit 51
bankrupt 93
banquet (n) 34
banquet   banqueted 133
bar   barred 182
barbecue 34
bare 70
barter   bartered 120
bask in   basked in 134
bath   bathed 125
batter   battered 150
battle 19
bawl   bawled 176
bazaar 46
beach 47
beacon 20
bear   bore 121
beast 2
beat   beat (defeat) 115
beat   beat (hit) 150
beautiful 94
become airborne   became airborne
    139
bedraggled 67
bedridden 80
beg   begged 114
began   *see* **begin**
beggarly 93
begin   began 116
beheld   *see* behold
behindhand 82
behold   beheld (see) 173
behold   beheld (watch) 194
belabour   belaboured 150
belated 82
bellow   bellowed 176

bench 13
bequeath   bequeathed 143
beseech   besought 114
besides 209
besought *see* beseech
bestow   bestowed 143
big 56
biography 49
bird 2
blackmail   blackmailed 168
blackmailer 51
blank 70
blaze (n) 20
blaze   blazed 175
blind alley 43
blissful 76
blistering (cold) 62
blistering (hot) 78
blitz 19
blubber   blubbered 128
boat 7
bold 58
bolt   bolted (close) 126
bolt   bolted (eat) 133
bolt   bolted (run) 144
bonfire 20
bony 105
book 8
bore   *see* bear
boring 57
borough 14
bothy 27
bottomless 66
bought   *see* **buy**
bound   bounded 152
box 9
boy 10
boyish 112
brainy 61
brake 54
brand   branded 119

brand-new 89
brat 4
brave 58
break   broke 117
break open   broke open 161
breed   bred 136
briefcase 5
brigand 51
bright (clean) 60
bright (clever) 61
bright (light) 84
brilliance 31
brilliant (clever) 61
brilliant (light) 84
brimful 75
brimming 75
bring   brought 121
briny 44
broad 111
broadcast   broadcast 174
broke   *see* **break**
broke (poor) 93
broken 59
broke open   *see* break open
brotherhood 38
brought *see* bring
brow 52
brush   brushed 188
budge   budged 159
buff   buffed 169
buffet   buffeted 150
build   built (construct) 118
build   built (make) 157
built *see* build
bulging 75
bulky 56
bullion 35
bunch 16
bungalow 27
buoyant 85
burgh 14

burglar 51
burgle   burgled 168
burn   burned 119
burning 78
burrow   burrowed 130
burst (adj) 59
burst   burst 117
bus 11
buxom 74
buy   bought 120
by-pass 43
by-path 43
by-road 43
by-way 43

C
cabinet 9
caddy 9
call 37
calling 29
came a cropper *see* come a cropper
came after   *see* come after
came by   *see* come by
came next   *see* come next
camouflage   camouflaged 149
campaign (fight) 19
campaign (war) 53
canoe 7
capable 61
caper   capered 152
capture   captured 122
car 12
care for   cared for 156
carefully 199
caress   caressed 188
carried *see* carry
carry   carried 121
cart-horse 26
carton 9
cartoon 39
cascade   cascaded 135

case (bag) 5
case (box) 9
cash 35
casket 9
cast   cast 187
castle 27
catapult   catapulted 187
catch   caught 122
catnap 48
caught   *see* **catch**
causeway 43
cautiously 199
cease   ceased 181
celebrated 72
chafe   chafed 169
chair 13
chalet 27
chance on   chanced on 137
chancy 63
chant   chanted 177
char   charred 119
charge (n) 40
charge   charged 170
charming 90
chase   chased (pursue) 123
chase   chased (run) 170
chat   chatted 184
cheer   cheered 176
cheerful 76
cheering 90
cherish   cherished 156
cherub 4
chest 9
child (baby) 4
child (boy) 10
child (girl) 24
childlike 112
chilly 62
choose   chose 124
chop   chopped 129
chore 29

chose *see* **choose**
chronicle (n) 49
chronicle   chronicled 196
chubby 74
chum 21
circumspectly 199
city 14
civil war 53
clamour   clamoured 176
clan 38
clasp   clasped 183
classic 8
clean (adj) 60
clean   cleaned 125
cleanse   cleansed 125
cleave   cleft 129
cleft *see* cleave
clever 61
clipper 45
cloak 15
close (adj) 108
close   closed 126
cloudburst 41
cluster   clustered 158
clutch   clutched 183
coach (n) (bus) 11
coach (teacher) 50
coach   coached 185
coast 47
coaster 7
coat 15
coinage 35
cold 62
collage 39
collapse   collapsed 135
colleague 21
colossal 56
colt 26
combat 19
come a cropper   came a cropper
  135

come after   came after 141
come by   came by 142
come next   came next 141
comfort (n) 25
comfort   comforted 148
comfortable 90
commence   commenced 116
comment   commented 172
community 38
companion 21
compensate   compensated 162
competent 61
competition 22
compose   composed (make) 157
compose   composed (write) 196
comprehend   comprehended 155
compressed 106
comrade 21
conceal   concealed 149
conclude   concluded 181
concluding 81
confer   conferred 143
conflagration 20
conflict 19
congregate   congregated 158
congregation 16
conquer   conquered 115
conscientiously 199
consequently 206
consider   considered (**see**) 173
consider   considered (**think**) 186
considerable 56
considerately 199
consign   consigned 174
constantly 198
construct   constructed (build) 118
construct   constructed (make) 157
consume   consumed (burn) 119
consume   consumed (use) 190
contact   contacted 188
container 9

contemplate   contemplated 186
content 76
contented 76
contest 22
continent 30
continually 198
continue   continued 180
continuously 198
contribute   contributed 143
convenient 69
converse   conversed 184
convertible 12
convey   conveyed 121
convey   conveyed 121
cool 62
copied *see* **copy**
coppice 54
copse 54
copy   copied 127
corner   cornered 146
corpulent 74
correct (adj) 99
correct   corrected 138
cost 40
cottage 27
couch 13
counsel counselled 148
country 30
county 30
coupé 12
courageous 58
cover up   covered up 149
crack   cracked 117
cracked (adj) 59
craft (boat) 7
craft (ship) 45
cram   crammed 185
crammed (adj) 75
crate 9
crave   craved 193
creak 37

create   created (build) 118
create   created (make) 157
creature 2
cremate   cremated 119
crest 52
cried *see* cry
cried out   *see* cry out
crisp 68
croft 18
crony 21
croon   crooned 177
crowd 16
crown 52
crumble   crumbled 117
crusade 53
crush (n) 16
crush   crushed 115
cry (n) 37
cry   cried 128
cry out   cried out 176
cul-de-sac 43
cultivate   cultivated 136
cure   cured 138
currency 35
cushiony 103
cut   cut 129

D
dab   dabbed 150
daily 204
damage   damaged 117
damp 110
damsel 24
dangerous 63
daring 58
dark 64
dash   dashed 170
dawdle   dawdled 191
daydream   daydreamed 186
daylight 31
dazzle (n) 31

dazzle dazzled 175
dazzling 84
dead 65
dead 65
debate debated 184
deceased 65
decimate decimated 154
deckchair 13
declaim declaimed (say) 172
declaim declaimed (talk) 184
declare declared 172
decoy decoyed 122
decrepit (ill) 80
decrepit (weak) 109
deep (n) 44
deep (adj) 66
defeat defeated 115
defunct 65
dehydrate dehydrated 132
dehydrated (adj) 68
dejected 100
deliberate 102
delighted 76
delightful 90
delightfully 202
deluge 41
demand demanded (ask) 114
demand demanded (want) 193
demanding 77
demised 65
demolish demolished 117
denied *see* deny
deny denied 182
depart departed 144
department store 46
deposit deposited 165
depressed 100
descend descended (fall) 135
descend descended (fly) 139
description 49
deserted 70

desiccated 68
desire desired 193
destitute 93
destroy destroyed 117
destroyed (adj) 59
destroyer 45
detached house 27
detain detained 153
detest detested 145
devotion 33
devour devoured 133
diagram 39
diary (book) 8
diary (story) 49
dictionary 8
difficult 77
dig dug (cultivate) 136
dig dug (excavate) 130
dilatory (late) 82
dilatory (slow) 102
dim 64
dine dined 133
dinghy 7
dingy 67
dirty 67
disappointed 100
discerning 61
discontented 100
discover discovered 137
disguise disguised 149
dislike disliked 145
dismal (dark) 64
dismal (sad) 100
dispatch dispatched 174
dispirited 100
dispute disputed 184
distinguished 72
district 30
dive dived 139
dog dogged 123
dogfight 19

donate   donated 143
double-decker 11
dovetail   dovetailed 151
downpour 41
downy 103
doze (n) 48
doze   dozed 179
drain   drained 132
dramatic 71
drank *see* drink
draught 17
drawing 39
dreary 100
drenched 110
dried *see* **dry**
drifter 7
drink (n) 17
drink   drank 131
dripping 110
drive (n) 43
drive   drove 159
drizzle (n) 41
drizzle   drizzled 166
drop   dropped 135
drove *see* drive
drowse   drowsed 179
dry (adj) 68
dry   dried 132
dry-clean   dry-cleaned 125
duel 19
duffelbag 5
duffelcoat 15
dug *see* dig
dull (boring) 57
dull (dark) 64
duplicate   duplicated 127
dusty 67
dwarf 86

E
earn   earned 142

easily 200
easy 69
eat   ate 133
eavesdrop   eavesdropped 147
echo   echoed (answer) 113
echo   echoed (copy) 127
educate   educated 185
effortless 69
effortlessly 200
eject   ejected 159
elated 76
elderly 91
elect   elected 124
elegant 94
elephantine 56
elope   eloped 144
embezzle   embezzled 168
embezzler 51
eminent 72
employ   employed 190
employment 29
emporium 46
empty 70
emulate   emulated 127
encounter   encountered 137
encyclopaedia 8
end   ended 181
endeavour   endeavoured 189
endlessly 198
endure   endured 180
engrave   engraved 195
enjoy   enjoyed 134
enjoyable 90
enjoyably 202
enlighten   enlightened 185
enormous 56
enquire   enquired 114
ensnare   ensnared 122
ensue   ensued 141
enterprising 58
entrap   entrapped 122

entreat   entreated 114
erect   erected (build) 118
erect   erected (make) 157
errand 29
escape   escaped 144
esplanade 43
establish   established 116
estate 30
estimate 40
eternally 198
evaporate   evaporated 132
event 22
everlastingly 198
evermore 198
everybody 1
everyone 1
everything 1
exact 99
examine   examined 178
excavate   excavated 130
exceedingly 210
exceptionally 210
excess 42
exciting 71
exclaim   exclaimed 176
exclude   excluded 182
excuse 3
execute   executed 154
expansive 111
expectant 97
expend   expended 190
expert 61
explanation 3
exploit   exploited 190
exquisite 94
exquisitely 210
extensive (big) 56
extensive (wide) 111
exterminate   exterminated 154
extinct 65
extra 87

extreme 81
extremely 210
extricate   extricated 171

F
fable 49
facile 69
fair 94
fairy-tale 49
fall   fell 135
famished 79
famous 72
fan 21
fantasy 49
fare 40
farm (n) 18
farm farmed 136
fascinating 71
fashion   fashioned 157
fast (adj) 73
fast (adv) 201
fat (big) 56
fat 74
fathomless 66
fearless 58
feast (n) 34
feast   feasted 133
featherweight 85
feathery 85
fed   see feed
fee 40
feeble 109
feed   fed 133
feel   felt 188
fell   see **fall**
fell   felled (cut) 129
felt   see feel
ferret out   ferreted out 137
ferried   see ferry
ferry   ferried 121
ferry-boat 7

fetch   fetched (carry) 121
fetch   fetched (take) 183
feud 19
feverish (hot) 78
feverish (ill) 80
fiery 84
fight (n) 19
file   filed 169
filly 26
filthy 67
final 81
finance 35
find   found 137
find out   found out 137
finish   finished 181
fire 20
fish 2
fit together   fitted together 151
fix   fixed 138
flabby 103
flail   flailed 150
flare 31
flash (n) 31
flash   flashed 175
flat 27
flay   flayed 150
fled   *see* flee
flee   fled (go) 144
flee   fled (run) 170
fleecy 103
fleet 73
flew   *see* **fly**
flicker   flickered 175
fling   flung 187
flog   flogged 150
flooded 110
flower-garden 23
flung   *see* fling
flush 98
fly   flew 139
fly   flew (move) 159

foal 26
folk 38
folk-tale 49
follow   followed (chase) 123, 140
follow   followed (come after) 141
fondness 33
fool about   fooled about 164
footpad 51
forbade   *see* forbid
forbid   forbade 182
forbidding 107
foreshore 47
forest 54
forge   forged 127
form   formed 118
formerly 208
formidable 77
forty winks 48
foul 67
found   founded 116
found *see* **find**
fracture   fractured 117
fractured (adj) 59
fragile 109
frail 109
freely 200
freezing 62
frequently 204
fresco 39
fresh 89
friend 21
friendship 33
frigate 45
frisk   frisked 164
frolic   frolicked 164
frosty 62
frozen 62
full 75
funds 35
further (adj) 87
further (adv) 209

fuse   fused 151

G
gabble   gabbled 184
gain   gained 142
galaxy 16
gallant 58
galleon 7
galley 7
gallop   galloped 170
gambol   gambolled (jump) 152
gambol   gambolled (play) 164
game 22
game park 55
gaping 92
garden 23
gash   gashed 129
gather   gathered 142
gaunt 105
gave *see* **give**
gaze at   gazed at (see) 173
gaze at   gazed at (watch) 194
get   got 142
ghastly 107
gifted 61
gigantic 56
girl 24
girlish 112
give   gave 143
glad 76
glance at   glanced at 173
glare (n) 31
glare   glared (shine) 175
glare at   glared at 173
gleam   gleamed 175
glide   glided 139
glimmer (n) 31
glimmer   glimmered 175
glimpse   glimpsed 173
glistening 84

glitter   glittered 175
glittering 84
globe 6
gloomy (dark) 64
gloomy (sad) 100
glorious 90
gloss 31
glow (n) 31
glow   glowed 175
go   went 144
go after   went after 141
gobble   gobbled 133
go next   went next 141
gorge   gorged 133
gormandize 133
gossip   gossiped 184
got *see* get
governess 50
grab   grabbed 183
graceful 94
gradual 102
grant   granted 143
grasp   grasped (know) 155
grasp   grasped (take) 183
gratifying 90
graze   grazed (cut) 129
graze   grazed (touch) 188
great 56
greatcoat 15
grew   *see* grow
grief-stricken 100
grimy 67
grind   ground 169
gripping 71
grisly 107
ground   *see* grind
group 16
grove 54
grow   grew (cultivate) 136
grow   grew (plant) 163
gruesome 107

guerrilla war 53
gulp   gulped 131
guru 50
gut   gutted 119
guzzle   guzzled (drink) 131
guzzle   guzzled (eat) 133

H
hack   hacked 129
had   *see* **have**
had fun   *see* have fun
hall 27
halt   halted 182
hammer   hammered 150
handbag 5
handbook 8
handle   handled 188
handy 88
hang about   hung about 191
hang out   hung out 132
happy 76
harangue   harangued 184
hard 77
hard up 93
hardy 104
harvest   harvested 136
hastily (fast) 201
hastily (suddenly) 207
hasty 73
hate   hated 145
have   had 146
have fun   had fun 164
haversack 5
hazardous 63
headmaster 50
headmistress 50
hear   heard 147
hearse 12
heave   heaved 187
heavy 74
held   *see* hold

held dear   *see* hold dear
held up   *see* hold up
help (n) 25
help   helped 148
herculean 104
heroic 58
hew   hewed (cut) 129
hew   hewed (make) 157
hibernate   hibernated 179
hibernation 48
hide   hid 149
hideous 107
highland 36
high seas 44
highway 43
highwayman 51
hill 36
hindmost 81
hint   hinted 172
historical 91
history 49
hit   hit 150
hobble   hobbled 192
hoe   hoed 130
hold   held 153
holdall 5
hold dear   held dear 156
hold up   held up 168
hollow (adj) 70
hollow   hollowed 130
hook   hooked 122
hop   hopped 152
horde 16
horrible 107
horse 26
host (crowd) 16
host (lot) 32
hostilities 53
hot 78
hound   hounded 123
house 27

hover   hovered 139
howl (n) 37
howl   howled 128
huddle 16
huge 56
hulking 56
hum   hummed 177
humanity 38
humdrum 57
hung about   *see* hang about
hung out   *see* hang out
hungry 79
hunt   hunted 123
hunter 26
hurl   hurled 187
hurried 73
hurriedly (fast) 201
hurriedly (suddenly) 207
hushed 95

I
icy 62
identify   identified 155
idle 83
idolize   idolized 156
ill 80
ill-omened 63
illumination 31
illustration 39
imagine   imagined 186
imitate   imitated 127
immature 112
immediately 203
immense 56
immortal 72
immune 101
impecunious 93
impede   impeded 182
impersonate   impersonated 127
implore   implored 114
impregnable 101

imprison   imprisoned 153
inanimate 65
inaugurate   inaugurated 116
incandescent 84
incessantly 198
increased 87
indisposed 80
indolent 83
infamous 72
infant 4
infirm 109
ingenious 61
initiate   initiated 116
inquire   inquired 114
inscribe   inscribed 195
insect 2
inspect   inspected 173
institute   instituted 116
instruct   instructed 185
instructor 50
intelligent 61
intensely 210
interesting 71
intrepid 58
invariably 198
invent   invented 157
invite   invited 114
invulnerable 101
in want 93
irksome 57
irresistible 104
island 28
island (land) 30
isle 28
islet 28

J
jalopy 12
jammed 106
jeep 12
jerkin 15

jihad 53
job 29
jog   jogged 170
join   joined 151
jot   jotted 196
joyful 76
joyless 100
joyous 76
jump   jumped 152
juvenile (n) boy 10
juvenile (n) girl 24
juvenile (adj) 112

K
keep   kept (have) 146
keep   kept 153
kept   *see* keep
kidnap   kidnapped (rob) 168
kidnap   kidnapped (take) 183
kidnapper 51
kill   killed 154
kill time   killed time 191
king-sized 56
kiosk 46
kitchen-garden 23
kleptomaniac 51
knew   *see* **know**
knock   knocked 150
know   knew 155

L
laborious 77
lacerate   lacerated 129
lack   lacked 160
lad 10
laid   *see* lay
land 30
landscape 39
lane 43
lanky 105
large 56

lash   lashed 150
lass 24
lassie 24
last (adj) 81
last   lasted 180
last-minute 82
late 82
late (dead) 65
lately 208
later 197
launch (n) 7
launch   launched (begin) 116
launch   launched (throw) 187
launder   laundered 125
lay   laid 165
lay down   *see* lie down
lazy 83
lean 105
leap   leaped 152
leave   left (give) 143
leave   left (go) 144
lecture   lectured (say) 172
lecture   lectured (talk) 184
lecture   lectured (teach) 185
lecturer 50
left *see* leave
legend 49
leisurely (adj) 102
leisurely (adv) 205
lie down   lay down 167
lifeless 65
light (n) 31
light (adj) (bright) 84
light (adj) (not heavy) 85
lightweight 85
like   liked (enjoy) 134
like   liked (love) 156
liking 33
limousine 12
limp (adj) 103
limp   limped 192

liner 45
linger   lingered 191
lingeringly 205
little 86
lively 73
loathe   loathed 145
local 88
locate   located 137
lock   locked 126
locker 9
locket 9
lodge 27
log 8
loiter   loitered 191
long for   longed for 193
look at   looked at (see) 173
look at   looked at (watch) 194
loot   looted 168
lope   loped 170
lot 32
love (n) 33
love   loved 156
lovely 94
lugubrious 100
lukewarm 108
luminous 84
lurch   lurched 192
lure   lured 122

M
mac 15
macintosh 15
made   *see* **make**
maiden 24
main 44
mainland 30
maisonette 27
make   made 157
mammal 2
mammoth 56

manageable 69
mangle   mangled 129
manipulate   manipulated 188
mankind 38
man-of-war 45
manor 27
manse 27
mansion 27
manual 8
manufacture   manufactured 157
manuscript 8
march   marched 192
mare 26
mark   marked 173
market 46
market-garden (farm) 18
market-garden (garden) 23
mart 46
mask   masked 149
massacre   massacred 154
massive 56
master 50
match 22
mate 21
mature 96
meagre 105
meal 34
medieval 91
meditate   meditated 186
meet   met 158
melée 19
memoirs 49
menacing 63
menagerie 55
mend   mended 138
mention   mentioned 172
merry 76
messy 67
met   *see* **meet**
meticulously 199
metropolis 14

microscopic 86
midget 86
mighty 104
mild 108
mimic   mimicked 127
mindfully 199
mine   mined 130
miniature 86
minicoach 11
minor (boy) 10
minor (girl) 24
minute 86
mirror   mirrored 127
miserable 100
mis-shapen 107
mission 29
mistress 50
mizzle   mizzled 166
mob 16
modern 89
moist 110
money 35
moneyed 98
monitor   monitored 147
monopolize   monopolized 146
monotonous 57
monsoon 41
monster 2
monstrous 107
moonlight 31
mop   mopped 125
more 87
moreover 209
moribund 65
mortally ill 80
mosaic 39
motorway 43
mount 26
mountain 36
mountainous 56
mouthful 17

move   moved (go) 144
move   moved 159
mucky 67
muddy 67
muggy 108
multitude (people) 16
multitude (things) 32
mumble   mumbled 184
mural 39
murder   murdered 154
murky 64
murmur (n) 37
murmur   murmured 184
muster   mustered 158
muted 95
myth 49
mythological 91

N
nap 48
narrative 49
nation 38
near 88
near-by 88
neat 94
need   needed 160
needy 93
neighbour 21
neighbouring 88
net   netted 122
new 89
new-fangled 89
next 88
nibble   nibbled 133
nice 90
nicely 202
nightcap 17
nimble 73
nip 17
nod   nodded 179
nod off   nodded off 179

noise 37
noiseless 95
notable 72
note   noted (see) 173
note   noted (write) 196
noted (adj) 72
notes 35
notice   noticed 173
notorious 72
novel (adj) 89
novel (book) 8
novel (story) 49
now 203

O
obese 74
oblige   obliged 148
obscure 64
observe   observed (say) 172
observe   observed (see) 173
observe   observed (watch) 194
obtain   obtained 142
ocean 44
occupation 29
occupy   occupied 146
often 204
old 91
old-fashioned 91
old master 39
ominous 63
once 208
onerous 77
opaque 64
open (adj) 92
open   opened 161
open out   opened out 161
open up   opened up 161
operate   operated 190
oppressive 78
optimistic 76

opulent 98
orate   orated 172
orchard 23
original 89
originate   originated 116
ornamental 94
overcame   see overcome
overcast 64
overcoat 15
overcome   overcame 115
overdue 82
overflowing 75
overhear   overheard 147
overheard   see overhear
overpower   overpowered 115
overpowering 104
overthrow   overthrew 115
overthrew   see overthrow
overweight 74
overwhelm   overwhelmed 115
overwhelming 104
own   owned 146

P
pace   paced 192
paid   see pay
paid attention to
        see pay attention to
paid for   see pay for
painless 69
palace 27
paperback 8
paper money 35
parable 49
parched 68
parish 30
parka 15
partner 21
passion 33
patch 23
path 43

prefab 27
prehistoric 91
prepared (for action) 97
prepared (for use) 96
present   presented 143
presently 208
preserve   preserved 153
press   pressed 188
pretty 94
prevent   prevented 182
price 40
principal 50
print (n) 39
print   printed 195
prise open   prised open 161
prize   prized 156
procure   procured 142
produce   produced 157
profession 29
professor 50
profound 66
profusion 32
prohibit   prohibited 182
prompt 73
promptly (now) 203
promptly (suddenly) 207
pronounce   pronounced 172
propel   propelled 159
protect   protected 171
protected (adj) 101
protection 25
protracted 57
provide   provided 143
province 30
prowl   prowled 192
public 38
publication 8
pummel   pummelled 150
punch   punched 150
purchase   purchased 120
purify   purified 125

pursue   pursued 123
pursuit 29
put   put (place) 165
put   put (throw) 187
put away   put away 153
put down   put down 165
put right   put right 138
put to death   put to death 154

Q
quatt   quatted 131
queue   queued 191
quick 73
quickly 201
quiet 95
quite 210
quotation 40

R
rabble 16
race 38
racehorse 26
racing-car 12
radiance 31
radiant 84
raid   raided 168
rain (n) 41
rain   rained 166
raise   raised 136
rally 22
ran   *see* run
ranch (n) 18
ranch   ranched 136
rant   ranted (say) 172
rant   ranted (talk) 184
rap   rapped 150
rapid 73
rapidly 201
rate 40

rave   raved 172
ravenous 79
raw 62
reach   reached 142
ready (for action) 97
ready (for use) 96
realize   realized (find) 137
realize   realized (know) 155
reap   reaped 136
rear (adj) 81
rear   reared 136
recent 89
recite   recited 172
recognize   recognized (know) 155
recognize   recognized (see) 173
recompense   recompensed 162
record   recorded 196
rectory 27
red-hot 78
reel   reeled 192
reflect   reflected 186
refreshing 90
refund   refunded 162
regard (n) 33
regard   regarded 173
regatta 22
region 30
reimburse   reimbursed 162
reinforce   reinforced 148
reinforcement 25
rejoinder 3
relax   relaxed 166
relief 25
relish   relished 134
remain   remained 180
remainder 42
remark   remarked 172
remarkably 210
remnant 42
remove   removed 144
rend   rent 117

rent   *see* rend
render   rendered 143
renowned 72
repaid   *see* repay
repair   repaired 138
repast 34
repay   repaid 162
repeat   repeated 127
repeatedly 204
repellent 107
replete 75
replied   *see* reply
reply (n) 3
reply   replied 113
report (n) 49
report   reported 196
repose   reposed 167
representation 39
reproduce   reproduced 127
reptile 2
repulsive 107
reputable 72
request   requested 114
require   required (need) 160
require   required (want) 193
rescue (n) 25
rescue   rescued 171
residue 42
resolute 58
respond   responded 113
response 3
rest (n) 42
rest   rested 167
restful 90
restore   restored 138
retail price 40
retain   retained (have) 146
retain   retained (keep) 153
retort (n) 3
retort   retorted 113
retrieve   retrieved 171

revel   revelled 164
revel in   revelled in 134
reward   rewarded 162
rich 98
riches 35
ridge 36
rifle   rifled 168
right 99
rinse   rinsed 125
ripe 96
riposte 3
rise   rose 139
risky 63
rivet   riveted 151
road 43
roar (n) 37
roar   roared 176
rob   robbed 168
robber 51
rocking-chair 13
rodent 2
romance 49
romp   romped 164
rose   *see* rise
rout   routed 115
route 43
rove   roved 192
rub   rubbed 169
rub   rubbed (touch) 188
rucksack 5
run   ran 170
rustle   rustled 168

S
sack (n) 5
sack   sacked 168
sacrifice   sacrificed 154
sad 100
saddlebag 5
safe (n) 9
safe (adj) 101

saga 49
said   *see* **say**
sail   sailed (fly) 139
sail   sailed (move) 159
saloon 12
salvage   salvaged 171
sang   *see* **sing**
sank   *see* sink
sat   *see* **sit**
satchel 5
satisfied 76
satisfying 90
satisfyingly 202
saturated (full) 75
saturated (wet) 110
saunter   sauntered 192
save   saved 171
saw   sawed (cut) 129
saw   *see* **see**
sawed   *see* saw
say   said 172
scald   scalded 119
scalding 78
scamper   scampered 170
scanty 105
schoolboy 10
schoolgirl 24
schooner 7
scintillate   scintillated 175
scorch   scorched 119
scorching 78
Scotch mist 41
scour   scoured 125
scourge   scourged 150
scrap 19
scrape   scraped 188
scrawl   scrawled 195
scrawny 105
scream (n) 37
scream   screamed 176
screech 37

screen   screened 149
scribble   scribbled 195
scrimmage 19
scrub (n) 54
scrub   scrubbed 125
scrutinize   scrutinized 173
scud 41
scuffle 19
scurry   scurried 170
sea 44
seal   sealed 126
search for   searched for 123
search out   searched out 123
seashore 47
seat 13
secrete   secreted 149
secure   secured (close) 126
secure   secured (get) 142
secure   secured (have) 153
secure (adj) 101
see   saw 173
seedy 80
seek   sought 123
seize   seized (catch) 122
seize   seized (take) 183
select   selected 124
self-service store 46
semi-detached house 27
send   sent 174
senile 91
sensational 71
sent   *see* **send**
serial 49
service 25
set down   set down 165
set right   set right 138
settee 13
settle 13
sever   severed 129
shack 27
shadow   shadowed (chase) 123
shadow   shadowed (follow) 141

shady 64
shampoo   shampooed 125
shape   shaped 157
shatter   shattered 117
shattered (adj) 59
shed tears   shed tears 128
sheltered 101
shielded 101
shift   shifted 159
shindy 19
shine   shone 175
shiny   clean 60
shiny (light) 84
ship (n) 45
ship   shipped (carry) 121
ship   shipped (send) 174
shivery 62
shocking 107
shone   *see* **shine**
shop 46
shoplifter 51
shore 47
shout   shouted (say) 172
shout   shouted 176
shovel   shovelled 130
shower   showered 166
shrewd 61
shriek 37
shuffle   shuffled 192
shut   shut 126
sick 80
siesta 48
sight   sighted 173
silent 95
silhouette 39
simple 69
simply 200
sing   sang 177
singe   singed 119
sink   sank 135
sip (n) 17
sip   sipped 131

sit   **sat** 178
situation 29
sizzling 78
sketch 39
skilful 61
skilled 61
skin   skinned 129
skinny 105
skirmish 19
slack 83
slam   slammed 126
slap   slapped 150
slash   slashed 129
slaughter   slaughtered 154
slay   slew 154
sleep (n) 48
sleep   **slept** 179
slender 105
slew   *see* slay
slice   sliced 129
slim 105
sling   slung 187
slit   slit 129
slothful 83
slovenly 67
slow 102
slowly 205
sluggish 102
sluggishly 205
slumber (n) 48
slumber   slumbered 179
slump   slumped 135
slung *see* sling
smack   smacked 150
small 86
smallholding 18
smart 61
smash   smashed 117
smashed (adj) 59
smoky 67
smooth   smoothed 169
smoothly 200

snack 34
snail-like 102
snap   snapped (break) 117
snap   snapped (say) 172
snare   snared 122
snatch   snatched 183
snooze (n) 48
snooze   snoozed 179
so 206
soaked 110
soar   soared 139
sob   sobbed 128
society 38
sodden 110
sofa 13
soft 103
soiled 67
solder   soldered 151
solution 3
sombre (dark) 64
sombre (sad) 100
soon 208
sooty 67
sorrowful 100
sought   *see* seek
sound 37
sow   sowed (farm) 136
sow   sowed (plant) 163
spacious (big) 56
spacious (wide) 111
spank   spanked 150
spare 105
sparkle   sparkled 175
sparkling 84
speak   spoke 172
speedily 201
speedy 73
sphere 6
spindly 105
spinney 54
splendid 94
splintered 59

split   split 117
splintered 59
split (adj) 59
spoil   spoiled 117
spoiled (adj) 59
spoke   *see* speak
sponge   sponged 125
spongy 103
sport   sported 164
sports 22
sports car 12
spotless 60
spout   spouted 184
sprang   *see* spring
spread 34
spring   sprang 152
spring-clean   spring-cleaned 125
sprint · sprinted 170
squalid 67
squat   squatted 178
stagger   staggered 192
stained 67
stainless 60
stalk   stalked 123
stall 46
stallion 26
stalwart 104
stand   stood 180
stand by   stood by (help) 148
stand by   stood by (wait) 191
stand fast   stood fast 180
stare at   stared at 173
start   started 116
starving 79
state (n) 30
state   stated 172
statement 49
stay   stayed 180
steal   stole 168
steed 26
steeped in 110

step   stepped 192
stifled 95
stifling 78
stimulating 71
stole   *see* steal
stood   *see* stand
stood by   *see* stand by
stood fast   *see* stand fast
stool 13
stop   stopped (cease) 181
stop   stopped (prevent) 182
store (n) 46
store   stored 153
story 49
stout (big) 56
stout (fat) 74
stout-hearted 58
strand 47
street 43
stride   strode 192
strike   struck 150
striking 71
stripling 10
strive   strove 189
strode   *see* stride
stroll   strolled 192
strong 104
strong-box 9
strove   *see* strive
struck   *see* strike
strut   strutted 192
stuck 106
study   studied 173
sturdy 104
stylish 94
submarine (boat) 7
submarine (ship) 45
subscribe   subscribed 143
subsequently 197
subside   subsided 135
suburb 14

succeed   succeeded 141
suck   sucked 131
suddenly 207
suitcase 5
sultry 78
sum (the) 1
summit 52
sunder   sundered 129
sunless 64
sunlight 31
sunny 108
sunshine 31
sup   supped 131
supermarket 46
support (n) 25
support   supported 148
supporter 21
suppress   suppressed 149
surplus 42
sustain   sustained 148
swagger   swaggered 192
swallow   swallowed (drink) 131
swallow   swallowed (eat) 133
swap   swapped 120
sweltering 78
swift 73
swiftly 201
swig (n) 17
swig   swigged 131
swill   swilled 131
swindler 51
swoop   swooped 139
swop   swopped 120

T
tag   tagged 123
tail   tailed 123
take   took (carry) 121
take   took 183
tale 49
talented 61

talk   talked 184
tanker 45
tap (n) 37
tap   tapped 150
tardy 82
tariff 40
tarnished 67
tarried   *see* tarry
tarry   tarried 180
task 29
taste (n) 17
taste   tasted (eat) 131
taste   tasted (drink) 133
taught *see* **teach**
taxi 12
teach   taught 185
teacher 50
tedious 57
teem   teemed 166
teenage 112
teenager 10
tender 7
tenderness 33
tepid 108
terminal 81
terraced house 27
territory 30
textbook 8
then (later) 197
then (at that time) 208
thereafter 197
therefore 206
thesaurus 8
thicket 54
thief 51
thieve   thieved 168
thin 105
think   thought 186
thirsty 68
thoroughbred 26
thought   *see* **think**

thoughtfully 199
thrash   thrashed 150
threatening 63
threw   *see* **throw**
thriller (book) 8
thriller (story) 49
thrilling 71
throne 13
throng   thronged 158
throng (n) 16
throw   **threw** 187
thump   thumped 150
thunderstorm 41
tickle   tickled 188
tight 106
till   tilled 136
tiny 86
tip   tipped 162
tipple (n) 17
tipple   tippled 131
tiresome 57
toast (n) 17
toast   toasted 131
toddle   toddled 192
toddler 4
tomboy 24
tome 8
tomorrow 208
too 209
took   *see* **take**
top 52
topped up 75
topple   toppled 135
tor 36
torrid 78
tortoise-like 102
toss   tossed 187
tot (baby) 4
tot (drink) 17
total (the) 1
total war 53

totter   tottered 192
touch   **touched** 188
tough 104
tournament 22
town 14
trace   traced 127
track (n) 43
track   tracked 123
trade 29
traditional 91
trail   trailed 123
train   trained 185
tram 11
tranquil 95
transmit   transmitted 174
transplant   transplanted 163
transport   transported 121
trap   trapped 122
travelogue 49
trawler 7
treacherous 63
treasure   treasured 156
tribe 38
tried   *see* **try**
trill   trilled 177
trolley-bus 11
tropical 78
trot   trotted 170
trounce   trounced 115
trudge   trudged 192
true 99
trunk 9
trunk road 43
try   tried 189
tuck in   tucked in 133
tug 7
tumble   tumbled 135
tunnel   tunnelled 130
tussle 19
tutor (n) 50
tutor   tutored 185

twinkle   twinkled 175

U
ugly 107
ultimate 81
unassailable 101
unceasingly 198
unclean 67
uncork   uncorked 161
uncover   uncovered 137
undefiled 60
undemanding 69
understand   understood 155
understood   *see* understand
unearth   unearthed 137
unerring 99
unexpectedly 207
unfenced 92
unfold   unfolded 161
unhappy 100
unhurried 102
unhurriedly 205
uninhabited 70
uninteresting 57
unite   united 151
unlit 64
unoccupied 70
unplumbed 66
unpunctual 82
unsightly 107
untainted 60
unwell 80
up-to-date 89
urchin 10
use   used 190
utilize   utilized 190
utter   uttered 172
utterly 210

V
vacant 70

valiant 58
value (n) 40
value   valued 156
vast 56
vault   vaulted 152
venerable 91
venture   ventured 189
vermin 2
very 210
vessel (boat) 7
vessel (ship) 45
vicarage 27
view   viewed (see) 173
view   viewed (watch) 194
vivarium 55
vocation 29
void 70
volume 8
vote for   voted for 124

W
waddle   waddled 192
wail (n) 37
wail   wailed 128
wait   waited 191
walk   walked 192
wallow in   wallowed in 134
want   wanted (need) 160
want   wanted (desire) 193
war (fight) 19
war 53
warble   warbled 177
warily 199
warm 108
wash   washed 125
washed (adj) 60
watch   watched 194
waterless 68
waterlogged 110
watery 110
waylay   waylaid 122

weak 109
wealth 35
wealthy 98
wearisome 57
wedged 106
wee 86
weep   wept 128
weightless 85
weld   welded 151
wench 24
went   *see* go
went after   *see* go after
went next   *see* go next
wept   *see* weep
wet 110
whimper (n) 37
whimper   whimpered 128
whine (n) 37
whip   whipped 150
whisper   whispered (say) 172
whisper   whispered (talk) 184
whole (the) 1
wholesale price 40
wide 111
wide-ranging 111
willowy 105
win   won 142
wintry 62
wipe   wiped 169
wiry 105
wise 61
wish for   wished for 193

withheld   *see* withhold
withhold   withheld 153
witness   witnessed 173
won   *see* win
wood 54
woodland 54
work 29
worship   worshipped 156
worth 40
write   wrote 195
write   wrote (compose) 196
write back   wrote back 113
wrote   *see* **write**
wrote back   *see* write back

Y
yacht 7
yarn 49
yawning 92
yell   yelled 176
yesterday 208
yielding 69
yodel   yodelled 177
young 112
youngster 10
youth 10
youthful 112

Z
zenith 52
zoo 55